Blockchain Technology:

Understanding the Technology behind Cryptocurrency, Blockchain's Limitless Potential and its Effects on Money and the World

David Vela

Table of Contents

Blockchain Technology: 1

Understanding the Technology behind Cryptocurrency, Blockchain's Limitless Potential and its Effects on Money and the World 1

Chapter 1 Introduction 4
How Transactions Are Verified 6
The Importance of Transparency in Transactions 7

Chapter 2 History of the Blockchain 8

Chapter 3 Basic Terms Used in Blockchain 14

Chapter 4 Components of the Basic Design of Blockchain 19

Chapter 5 Harnessing Global Integrity 23

Chapter 6 The Issue of Trust within Blockchain 26

Chapter 7 The Blockchain Revolution 32

Chapter 8 Benefits of the Blockchain Technology 39

Chapter 9 Disadvantages of Using Blockchain Technology 44

Chapter 10 The Role of Blockchain Technology in Future Capital Markets 52

Chapter 11 Building a Mining Rig 62

Chapter 12 Blockchain Technology Myths 71

Conclusion 76

Chapter 1 Introduction

Although most people automatically believe blockchain and bitcoin are the same thing, the reality is that bitcoin is only a manifestation of blockchain. Blockchain is essentially the platform that enables bitcoin, as well as other cryptocurrencies, to exist. Without it, these currencies would not have any basis and therefore they would not be usable.

Blockchain is essentially a decentralized database system that can store transaction data distributed across many different nodes. Because of the fact that it is decentralized, you do not actually have to physically travel to a location in order to complete a transaction. Instead, you can engage in the transaction virtually anywhere.

To break it down, imagine that you want to deposit money into your bank account. As a result, you visit your local branch and deposit the money. At that time, a transaction takes place and is recorded by the bank after they verify the authenticity of the payment. Your account is then updated to reflect the new deposit, and the money becomes available to you electronically.

Based on the current methods of transactions, the bank is inevitably always going to be involved. Even when you are processing a debit transaction at a retail location, the bank is involved in the process. Aside from the frustrations associated with having to have a third party present with everything, banks also carry other problems. Despite the amount of work that goes into keeping them secure and preventing manipulation, it cannot be completely manipulated. Additionally, that work itself is a drawback as it is costly to audit the banks and ensure that no manipulation is taking place. The current procedures are slow, can hold a variety of different errors, and are not completely safe from system tampering. Ultimately, they are becoming outdated.

The more society grows, the more important our currencies become. They are the basis for everything we do in life, whether we like to admit it or not. Even individuals who choose to live "off the grid" and attempt to avoid modern society are forced to use currency in order to acquire the things they need for their off-grid residencies. There is no denying the importance of currency. With currency comes transactions, and understandably you are going to want to have effective programs and systems in place to secure your transactions and ensure that there is no manipulation or tampering taking place with your money.

Blockchain is a program that has revolutionized the way transactions take place. It removes the requirement for third-party facilitators in transactions. Also, unlike banks where names and other potentially sensitive information is shared, blockchain maintains a level of anonymity to ensure that both parties involved in the transaction are further secured from any type of manipulation or tampering. Based off of the systems in place with blockchain, the transaction is authenticated, validated, and then approved and takes place. There are a series of cryptographic data signals that are involved in completing the transaction which makes it permanently approved and, in essence, completed. Then, the data is "hashed" onto the ledger of said node to form a chain of transaction records which cannot be hidden or erased.

The series of having the transactions stored on a chain where they cannot be erased adds an entire layer of security on its own. Due to the inability to erase or hide the chain, anyone who attempts to engage in fraudulent or illegal activities will be stopped immediately and the transaction will not take place. Ultimately, it is a completely secure foundation for transactions to take place.

How Transactions Are Verified

Blockchain has an ability to provide a high level of transparency behind transactions. Whenever transactions are verified by a node, every other node in the blockchain system is notified and therefore no transaction can be kept a secret. Every single node will have its system updated with the recent transaction, and it will not be possible to erase or hide the transaction. It will forever be linked to said person's name or code. Because all nodes are in agreeance with each other based on their histories, it is impossible to build a lie around a transaction, since they are clearly maintained and visible.

This is important because it is basically impossible to corrupt blockchain or commit fraud on the blockchain system. You cannot redirect payments to alternative accounts for money laundering, double-spend your money, or in any way increase the amount of money that is transferred to you or any other individual in any fraudulent way. Committing fraudulent activity on blockchain is virtually impossible to accomplish, and it is believed that it cannot be done. Aside from all of the technical complexities that would arise when you attempt to hack a node, you would not be able to change the transaction based on the decentralized program that blockchain is built on. There are several nodes that the transactions are inputted into, and you cannot change all of them through a single node. If you were able to hack a node and change a transaction on the node, the other nodes on the system would recognize the disagreement and the transaction would be halted as a result.

The entire system is also public, so anyone can see what has been done based on the transaction chains.

The Importance of Transparency in Transactions

Because of how blockchain functions, there is major transparency among all of the transactions that take place. All of these transactions can be located on a database that is viewable by the public, therefore all attempts at money laundering and committing fraudulent activities will be greatly reduced by the system. Any type of corruption around currency would be easily exposed and therefore it would be more difficult for large corporations and government to commit the fraud or corruption without being caught by the public. It ultimately democratizes the knowledge around transactions, which can have the ability to lead to more efficient markets.

At first, it may seem confusing to understand blockchain. It is a rather complex program that has taken computer scientists, mathematicians and cryptographers about a decade to compile. Rather than needing to understand the complexities of blockchain, the most important thing for you to understand is the way it works, how you can profit from it, and why blockchain is a revolution in and of itself. Understanding how powerful blockchain is and the number of changes it can make to modern society is important because it can assist you in understanding exactly why blockchain is important.

Chapter 2 History of the Blockchain

Although Satoshi Nakamoto, the creator of Bitcoin, takes home the trophy for creating the first widely accepted application using the blockchain technology, blockchain has a long history that came before him (he still takes home the trophy for creating the first usable form of blockchain. In fact, most of the applications using this technology today use what he was able to achieve as a benchmark).

In 1991, Stuart Haber and W. Scott Stornetta wrote a paper describing a cryptographically secure chain of block. In the following year, as a way to improve the efficiency of the ability to collect several of the documents into a block, the two introduced Merkle trees.

In 2008, Satoshi Nakamoto conceptualized the first distributed form of the blockchain. In the following year, he implemented it to create the currency Bitcoin. In Bitcoin, the blockchain served the purpose of being the management mechanism for the publicly distributed ledger for all financial transactions between peers. In this regard, the system used the peer-to-peer modeling and a distributed timestamp to make sure that the management of the Bitcoin database remained autonomous. The use of blockchain in the creation of Bitcoin proved the key to solving the problem of double spending, something very common with digital currencies in those days, without the need for secure administration.

In his initial paper published on 2008, Satoshi (the identity of Satoshi is still unknown. Some think he is a man living in Japan while others consider Satoshi a pseudonym for a group), used the terms block and chain on separate occasions and as separate terms. When others started using what he had achieved, they used the term block chain and in 2016, the term became one: blockchain.

In 2014, just six years after the conceptualization of Bitcoin, the first app running on the blockchain technology (Bitcoin and blockchain are not mutually exclusive and as you now know, Bitcoin is not the only use of the blockchain technology), the size of the Bitcoin blockchain stood at over 20 gigabytes. As use of the currency increased, the size of the file increased to over 30 gigabytes by January of the following year (2015), a size that had grown to over 100 gigabytes by 2017.

2014 brought with it a new term: blockchain 2.0, a term used to refer to applications (other than Bitcoin) using the blockchain technology called Ethereum. An Op-ed piece published on The Economist described the implementation of these new generation apps as follows: "blockchain 2.0 is a sort of programming language that allows users to write sophisticated smart contracts. These smart contracts allow for the creation of invoices that pay themselves upon the arrival of a shipment or share certificates that automatically send their owners dividends if profits reach a certain level."

While this definition is very true, application of blockchain 2.0 applications goes beyond transaction. They allow for the exchange of value on a peer-to-peer basis without the explicit need of powerful intermediaries such as banks acting as arbiters or keeping records of transactions or information. These applications allow those who would otherwise not have access to global currencies such as the dollar or pound to play an equal part in global trade and economy. Through smart contracts and cryptography, these platforms also foster privacy protection (which is why in its early days, criminals on the Silk Road website used Bitcoin as their preferred means of trade).

Applications that use blockchain 2.0 make the storage of a person's individual ID and persona easier and secure; because of this, they are helping shape future monies, distribution of wealth, and ease wealth inequality.

A Chronological Development of Blockchain Related Technologies

We cannot fail to mention that in the 10 years the blockchain innovation has been in existence, it has gone through some changes and seen the introduction of various new technologies that have made it what it is today. Here is a chronological view of these changes:

1. The first major innovation of the technology occurred when Satoshi introduced Bitcoin, the first successful application to use the blockchain technology. Introduced in a world in dire need of a decentralized currency, wide adoption of Bitcoins has seen their market cap rise to over $20 billion. Today, thousands of people across the world are using this blockchain-based currency to make payments and online purchases.

2. After the development of Bitcoin came the realization that the underlying technology could apply to many other areas and that the technology itself was not synonymous with Bitcoins. Many world-leading financial institutions are currently researching how they can integrate the technology into their financial offerings and in-house applications. According to research by Fortune.com, about 15% of all major banks are looking into how they can integrate the technology into their processes.

3. The third major innovation in blockchain development was the introduction of smart contracts. Simply put, a smart contract is a computer-based protocol whose aim is to

facilitate, enforce, and verify contractual negotiations. Of all smart contracts introduced, the Ethereum blockchain platform is the most prominent one; we shall discuss its development and application later. Ethereum built multiple, 2nd gen programs into the blockchain platform to allow for the transfer of loans, bonds, and other financial instruments. The development of Ethereum came out of necessity.

4. The 4th innovation, which is what many blockchain 2.0 applications in existence today use, is proof of stake. Applications such as Bitcoin (the current version of it), use something called proof of work. In the blockchain world, proof of work is data that is easy to verify based on certain requirements but that is difficult or costly to produce. Proof of work produced the aspect of mining where a computer or group of networked computers with the most computing power would make the decisions in that since they had the most power, they could provide secure proof of work faster for all blockchain transactions such as cryptocurrencies transfers or payments. For their services, these computers earn cryptocurrencies; this explains why cryptocurrency mining has become popular.

These four are the main developmental stages of blockchain. Experts also agree that in the days to come, another revolutionary innovation that is going to change the blockchain technology is blockchain scaling. Here is how this shall pan out.

We have already established that a blockchain is a decentralized, peer-to-peer managed ledger upon which the transactions recorded by the computers on the network reside. As we have also seen, processing these transactions uses the computing power of every computer in the network, something that has proven slow and rather expensive to manage (which is why cryptocurrency mining is not as lucrative as it once used to be).

Because of the above, blockchain scaling, a new form of blockchain innovation, is on the horizon. This innovation intends to accelerate the rate at which the computers on the network record the data into blocks, all this without sacrificing the security or integrity of the block. To do this, blockchain scaling intends to interrogate the network to determine the number of computers needed to validate individual transactions and using this base number, divide the work equally among all the computers in the network. As you can imagine, this will lead to increased efficiency. This technology, if it comes to fruition, which is likely to be very soon, will rival technologies such as SWIFT and VISA, and play an integral role in powering the internet of things.

The above is a representation of how blockchain has changed in the last 10 years thanks to the work of an elite group of mathematicians, cryptographers, and computer scientists working to improve this disruptive innovation. As the innovation continues to improve, it is changing many things about how we live our everyday life. For instance, many experts in the field opine that as these breakthroughs come through, the future may see us using blockchain technologies to pay for services such as charging stations and landing pads for self-driving cars and drones.

Now that we are talking about how the blockchain technology is changing the future of money, we cannot fail to discuss Ethereum, the other blockchain innovation that is changing our perception of the blockchain as a predominantly currency-development technology. Before we do that, however, let us discuss the benefits of the blockchain technology.

Chapter 3 Basic Terms Used in Blockchain

Before we plunge straight into the other essential information about the blockchain, let me familiarize you with some of the commonly used basic terms in blockchain. These terms may be defined again in some chapters, but I decided to compile them in one chapter, as a quick reference.

Blockchain

A public or private ledger distributed to people in the blockchain's network.

Peer-to-Peer (P2P) networking

A decentralized network, where peer-to-peer (direct user to user) transactions occur, without the mediation of a third party.

Public Key

This is a cryptograph or code utilized by a blockchain user to verify that the other user is the actual person he is dealing with. It's used to verify the user's private key.

Private Key

This is a cryptograph or code that can verify that the user is definitely who he claims he is. You can use your private key to access your wallet where your cryptocurrency is stored. If you lose this key, you cannot enter your black box or wallet, thus, you will lose private data and your digital money as well. Subsequently, you can create another black box, but you can never recover your money in the original box, if you don't have your own private key.

Node

You and your computer are nodes because you are the one running, reading, writing and downloading blocks through your own computer.

Proof-of-work (PoW)

Proof-of-work is accomplished when a miner solves a math problem. When this is done, the new block is added to the chain. Miners are usually paid in digital currency as incentives in solving the problem. When the majority of the nodes in the network approves of the solution, all the nodes are updated with the new block. PoW also grants a 'right' to participate in the blockchain network.

Proof-of-stake (PoS)

This is intended to be an alternative for proof-of-work. It's a consensus algorithm, that stems from the holdings of the cryptocurrency. PoS eliminates the 51% attack. The 51% attack involves the acquisition of 51% computing power by a hacker, and then using this to control the network. This is almost impossible, however, because the bitcoins in circulation are not equal to 51% of Bitcoin. Between PoW and PoS, PoS is tougher to compromise.

Transaction

A transaction deals with assets, usually financial, that blockchain users engage in. But asset may not concern only money but anything of value to the users (data, information, properties (tangible and intangible), and similar items.

Contract

This is an agreement that details the condition of the transaction between users. It specifies the business terms or what is expected from both parties. If the expectations are not fulfilled, the process of what would happen must be itemized and explicitly stated, so that it can be executed automatically.

Hash

A hash is used to connect the new block to the previous block to make it tamper-proof. All blocks are 'hashed' together to ensure the validity, legitimacy and trueness of the block. In short, it acts as a unique digital fingerprint. Hash codes are used to secure transactions through cryptography.

Cryptocurrency

This is the currency (digital money) used in blockchain transactions, where encryption of algorithms confirms the transactions.

Digital currency

This is the currency used in online transactions. It may not be necessarily a cryptocurrency.

Assets

Assets can be tangible (house, car, store) and intangible (music, stories, bonds, patents), and are usually used in blockchain transactions. These are items that can produce value that can be owned by users.

Ledger

This is where transactions are recorded. In blockchain, the shared ledger is the same. It's also where blockchain transactions are recorded. Only, it's now shared and distributed to all members of the network.

Block

This is considered a 'page' where permanent files are recorded. They are usually in chronological order, according to time. These connecting blocks make up the blockchain.

Consensus

Consensus is the general agreement of the users about the validity of a block, or a solution to an issue. This ensures that the blockchain is protected because of the provision of exact copies to all users in the blockchain network. This is done through the shared ledgers. Any tampering of the blocks can be confirmed if the block doesn't appear simultaneously in all the distributed ledgers. Consensus is said to have been reached, if all the blocks in all shared and distributed ledgers are identical.

Decentralization

This is the process of eliminating intermediaries and spreading the power or responsibility among all users of a blockchain network. This denotes that no one owns the chain, and not any one person can control it.

Internet of Things (IoT)

This encompasses the continuously growing interconnection of a global network of physical and virtual devices or apps and the values/assets or data they communicate to each other on the Internet.

These are some terms that you may come across with when you are reading about blockchain. This is not complete because there are numerous terms involving blockchain, but these are the most common.

Chapter 4 Components of the Basic Design of Blockchain

All platforms using the blockchain technology is recommended to have the major components of its basic design. This is due to the fact that the blockchain involves value transfer and the exchange of valuable data or information.

For blockchain to be a success, these components must be present in its basic design. These include the following:

Security

Blockchain can never operate without adequate security. Its design is made in such a way that the design becomes a security feature in itself.

Nonetheless, in this era of Internet explosion and state-of-the-art technology, there will always be issues about security. Premier banks worry about their security. Well-known websites worry about their security. In other words, it's an unending and widespread problem.

Therefore, blockchain is no exception. Most private blockchain platforms/systems are adding extra features to the existing blockchain security to ensure that their systems are secure.

Privacy

The privacy of users is protected through the use of public and private keys. You can refer to the previous chapters on how these keys (secret codes) are generated and used, and how privacy is protected with the use of the black box. The black box is where all the user's private information and data are stored. Only the user with his blockchain ID can access his blackbox. An example of a blockchain ID is 9b3cae0-67b1-56gc-a3c7-g328a2bcfcf7. This is entered together with the password, before a user can access his blockchain account.

Network Integrity

The integrity of your network is essential for a blockchain system to succeed. The trust protocol is what develops a network that you can trust. Each node must be honest, and expects other nodes to be honest as well. The strength of a blockchain lies in its weakest link.

Decentralization

Decentralization is one of the vital advantages of blockchain. This process allows network users to have control over their assets, and to trade, sell, or do whatever they wish - without the interference of mediators. In this regard, all the users in the blockchain network are on equal footing.

Financial Inclusion

This deals with users who have no bank accounts for various reasons. They have to be included in the blockchain network. There are billions of people using the Internet who still don't have basic bank accounts because they lack documents, such as birth certificates, that could support their identity. It could also be because they don't have the amount of money needed for an initial deposit. Whatever the reason, you have to make sure that 'inclusion' is one of the features of the blockchain.

Using blockchain so that these people can be included in the network will be advantageous to both the concerned countries and the 'unbanked' people.

In the absence of a computer, people can use mobile phones to connect to the blockchain. Mobile banking is largely recognized by almost all countries, and the inclusion of a blockchain in the banks' systems would allow these 'unbanked' people to be able to open accounts without presenting documents.

The inclusion need not be financial only. It could also be in other aspects of society, where people need to transact business - but could not, because they lack proper documentation, or pertinent papers (example: refugees).

Blockchain can allow users to create their digital identity without their proper documents.

With these in mind, it's safe to conclude that the blockchain system can create a new world, where everyone can be included and be fairly treated. Inequality will be eschewed because everyone has equal opportunities in the network. This system will encourage an open, fair and inclusive economy, thus, has the propensity of wealth redistribution.

Rights preserved

Each user's right must be preserved by the blockchain. Each member of the blockchain is an important block in the chain. If one is broken, all the other blocks will be disconnected, affecting the entire blockchain. Therefore, the rights of each member must be preserved and respected.

Value as incentive

In some blockchain platforms, incentives are given to miners. These incentives come in the value of cryptocurrencies or digital money. Most blockchain sites have similar rules with regards to granting incentives using their own digital coins.

Since the open source code of the blockchain technology has become available to the public for free, numerous sites/platforms have sprouted and used the code. Some of them have modified or developed the blockchain to suit their purposes. The basic components, though, must be integrated.

Chapter 5 Harnessing Global Integrity

For blockchain to work properly, integrity should exist between users. Bear in mind that there are no third parties to mediate. Hence, each user must be responsible and honest with his transactions. This can be possible with the establishment of global integrity. This means that every user around the world is watching all the transactions that are done. So, it would be difficult to intentionally commit mistakes with the purpose of deceiving another user.

For all digital transactions, each blockchain user is expected to adhere to the principles of integrity.

What is integrity?

Integrity is the ability or quality to be true, honest and accurate about one's deeds. It indicates the ethical and moral responsibility of a person to himself and to other people.

How can integrity be demonstrated in blockchain transactions?

The integrity of the user can be demonstrated through his honesty, transparency, accountability and concern for other users in his dealings. Honesty is being upfront with what the other user can benefit or lose from the transaction.

On the other hand, transparency is the trait of being able to allow the other users to see the transactions you are doing in your own node. This doesn't mean that all users can see your personal and private information, remember, these are encrypted. What other users can see, is the summary of your transaction.

Accountability is to be held responsible for contracts agreed on, or being able to take responsibility for the consequences of one's actions. Concern about the other users can focus on the law of 'karma'. 'What goes around comes around' is an apt cliché to describe this behavior. 'Karma' is a law of nature. You will surely receive what you have 'given' to other people.

The rule of 'karma' can be demonstrated in this simple occurrence. Throw a stone into a stagnant lake and observe how the ripples of waves go outwards, and then back inwards again. In this regard, each user must not attempt to rip off other users, if he doesn't want to be ripped off in return.

When all blockchain users observe these traits, then cryptocurrency transactions will become a resounding success.

How does transparency occur in blockchains?

When I talk about transparency, I'm talking about transparency in your digital transactions. It's understandable that extremely private information or data are not revealed to other users. Only, what you want to be disclosed will be shown. How can this be done? You can create your digital business persona, or another persona that will deal with other aspects of your blockchain transactions. All your personal information is placed in a special box, which you can monetize any way you want. For example, you can monetize your data about your favorite movies by participating in an online survey.

To secure your identity, a specific 'key' is assigned to you, and only you can open your box with that key. So, you control the revelation of your information. With that unique 'key', blockchain helps you protect your identity.

While protecting your identity, you are expected to participate actively as a node. You and your computer constitute a node. Say for example on Bitcoin, as a node in a public blockchain, you can do the following:

- Download and store the blockchain free core software
- Listen, validate and pass on transactions
- Listen, validate and pass on blocks
- Mine and create blocks

Your transactions are secured using the public key and your own private keys. Bear in mind that the security of your private key is your responsibility alone. You should not divulge it to anyone. Your previous transactions will serve as another method to confirm your identity.

Also, you can prevent hackers from stealing your blockchain account by: adding a phone number and email address, so that when there are changes, you can be notified promptly. Use the two-factor authorization/authentication too, where you have to add an extra password.

As more global users transact their businesses on blockchain, global integrity can be gradually achieved.

Chapter 6 The Issue of Trust within Blockchain

The issue of trust in blockchain is critical to its success. Since the onset of the Internet, online transactions have increasingly spiraled. This is done through the assistance of third parties, such as PayPal and similar companies. The trust established with these companies was teetering though, because of the danger of private and personal information being compromised or leaked by hackers.

This is not only true in financial companies but also on social media sites. Reportedly, Facebook alone has more than 300 petabytes of private information from its users. For now, Facebook (FB) has successfully protected the private data of its users.

However, if you notice the ads being displayed when you sign in into your account, you will know that FB knows your interests and preferences. It's monetizing your private information legally, and it's earning big money from these data. This is why it's possible for FB to provide incredible apps in its site and provide them to you – for free.

In blockchain, the problem of your private information being disclosed won't likely occur anymore. This is because the transactions are conducted only between the persons doing the transactions - without the assistance of third parties. You can now monetize your own information too, if you want. It's up to you.

But how does blockchain ensure security within its technology? How can it ascertain that the user's identity and private information is secure and safe? How can you trust blockchain and how can other blockchain users trust you?

1.   First, to gain trust, you must be trustworthy.

The transactions you conduct, your location, and the contacts you deal with are evidences of your identity. You may not be aware of it but you leave your 'footprints' around the Internet with your comments, your posts, your membership in sites, your searches, the videos you watch, the games you play, your time stamps, and similar activities. These are all 'recorded' by the World Wide Web and taken advantage of by big companies to earn money. Your digital identity comes from your online activities.

In the blockchain technology, users, as nodes, are expected to be trustworthy. If you're not trustworthy, other users can see your wrongdoing. It's like you're playing on the world stage where your every movement is recorded, and every one can see what you're up to. So, you cannot change entries, or enter into spurious transactions without anyone noticing the activity on the real-time worldwide ledger.

As you do more transactions with other users and establish more relationships, your identity grows together with your trustworthiness. It is believed that the more you pour work into the system, the less likely you'll cheat. Hence, you as a node in the blockchain, becomes a legitimate measure of other nodes that you associate with.

2.   In blockchain, YOU control your own data using a private key.

You can use as many pseudonyms as you want. Every time you perform a transaction, you are asked to enter your personal private 'key', known only to you. In essence, there are two keys that you have to use. The first is the public key, which can correspond to your user ID, when you sign in to regular sites, and the private key, which can correspond to your password. However, it's not as simple as it appears. These public and private keys are not as easy as using your user ID and password. Examples of the public keys are SHA256 (reportedly used by US government) and RIPEMD160.

The keys are cryptographic (cipher text) in nature that is unreadable to viewers. Only you, as the user, or owner of the data can decrypt the cipher text to a readable form using your private key. You should keep your private key a secret, but you can reveal your public key.

You can call this the black box or your personal wallet, which contains all your pertinent and private information.

3. The use of the Trust Formula.

Some blockchain private users have created a Trust Formula that is used to compute for the trust score for every node in the blockchain. This formula is based on the blockchain's purpose. Generally, random nodes are selected to be used in the formula. The formula involves the good and bad actions the user (node) performs, and then turning this into a probability through the sigmoid function.

The sigmoid function or sigmoidal curve is a logistic (planning or implementation) mathematical function that usually takes an S- shape curve.

This may start to sound so technical, so, I'll simply say, that these sigmoid curves can illustrate progress of innovations, business cycles and to 'squash' (reduce into a small number) responses to keep the data within bounds and come up with a probability. This will then provide a clue into the trustworthiness of the node (user).

I would like to present the formula, but I know it would confuse some readers, so I'll skip it. Anyway, you won't be computing the formula yourself, the blockchain technology will do it for you - automatically.

To give you a visual picture of what a blockchain is, you can imagine an endless, interconnected chain that goes on and on. As they are interconnected with each other; you cannot remove or alter one chain without affecting all the other blocks. Since it's also public, anyone can see whatever alterations are being done. The bad node will have to alter everything from the start of the chain until the current block, which is nearly impossible. The link is growing faster and longer that the bad node won't be able to catch up.

4. Tamper-proof distributed ledgers and identity

As explained earlier the blockchain acts as a public world ledger, and the data entered are immutable (unchangeable). Users cannot tamper with the data because they are interconnected to each other, up to the very first transaction. The ledgers are distributed too, to each user, so any changes would be updated real-time into all of the distributed ledges, hence, it could not be altered. It's like – each node in the block has the ability to look out for each other. Your identity is also tamper-proof (please refer to the previous discussions).

5. Use of several codes and hashes

In addition, Blockchain codes are used in securing the users' privacy through the use of cryptography. There's a code used in generating a compound identity; another code is used in gaining permission for entry into the blockchain; the third code is for the access control protocol; and the fourth code for the loading and storing of data.

In the event that another person tries to change or utilize another user's private key, the hash will act as a trap to stop the process. The hashes should match to ensure that the message is not altered and that the key is correct. If the hash is altered, it indicates that the private key is wrong. Only your key can encrypt the hash of the message to confirm or sign that you own the message.

6. Use of Smart Contracts

This is a computer programmable code contained in the blockchain, which can be executed when the user fulfills certain conditions. This is one way that the blockchain in bitcoin and other platforms protect and secure the data and identity of users or nodes. These contracts are replicated and shared in the ledger that is available to all users.

Reportedly, there were instances in the past, in which tests were done to introduce unrelated data to the blockchain using bots, or software turned into malware. This is one possibility that can introduce potential harm to the blockchain security system. This development will surely prompt blockchain users to develop more technology, on top of the blockchain technology, to ensure that the security of the information provided and the identity of the nodes (users) are safe.

In addition, in blockchain, trust is established using mass consensus or confirmation, plus, the utilization of clever codes that have to be decrypted.

Chapter 7 The Blockchain Revolution

The future of blockchain is the essence of the blockchain revolution. In just one decade, it has come incredibly far and has left so many changes in its path. Like the internet or the smartphone, blockchain is a system that is believed to be heading in a direction that will make massive changes to our entire way of life. You will likely find that blockchain will change everything from the way we sell art and products to the way we manage finances and purchase goods. There are many ways that blockchain technology can have a major impact on our future.

As we have discussed periodically throughout this book, blockchain has the ability to bring about a great amount of security with it. Because of this, there is a huge potential to greatly reduce the risks attached to the online space. Identity authentication will be offered through a public ledger that makes it easier for people to be caught when they are committing fraudulent activities. There are already requirements attached around numbering, maintaining and indexing records around transactions, and the information that is provided in the records need to be communicated from time to time, as well. This is especially true when you are working with different financial services to assist you with certain activities. Having a blockchain system storing all of this information would make it more easily accessible, as well as it would increase the security and efficiency around the storing of the information.

There are many other things that can be controlled, as well. For example, if blockchain technology was more widespread, pieces of physical property could be attached to the blockchain system and could perform incredible functions on its own. Fridges, for example, could be equipped with sensors that allow them to order and pay for food, as well as arrange software upgrades. In addition, it could track its own warranty, so if something was wrong it would be able to make a claim and then the appropriate servicing department would come out to assist you in fixing your fridge. This could be true for many things, beyond just fridges. Cars could be hybridized and parked on specific parking pads that would charge them, and they would automatically pay for their charges. Your car could track its own warranties and any things associated with it that may need to be repaired or fixed. There are several items that could benefit from being connected to a blockchain system with sensors and internet connection. This type of connection would enable many of your pieces of technology to be self-sufficient and would require minimal maintenance on your behalf to keep the system functioning properly.

On a business end, small businesses would have the ability to use the sophisticated blockchain technology to create their own trusted trading platforms which they could then trade among other small businesses. The corporate trading industry would no longer be restricted to only large corporations, but rather any business who wanted to get involved. This would open up a great opportunity to help bring transparency to the trading environment, especially the post-trade section. Based on the speed of blockchain technology, the timing associated with investment risks would be completely altered. Trading as we know it would be completely different from what it is now.

Another reason why the speed of blockchain would be incredible is that it would alter the speed at which the bank is able to pay suppliers. Payments could be made instantly, which could make the rate at which things are done much quicker. People would no longer have to wait for transactions to be approved and authenticated and then released because these fulfillments would be done instantly.

Blockchain would also have a major impact on crime. Based on the methodology behind blockchain, there are people who are claiming that they can use this system to track down criminals faster than ever. Additionally, this service would be cheaper than existing tracking services. There would be less waiting to catch criminals and fewer criminals on the streets being left to their own devices. Anyone who committed a crime would be much more likely to be identified, caught, and forced to serve their justice.

There are some complications that arise when it comes to integrating blockchain with banks. These risks are currently the reason why many banks have hesitated to get completely on board with the new system. Many banks, however, are investing in learning more about these technologies to see how they can alter the risk and turn it into a positive. If banks were to adopt blockchain technology, it is not surprising that cryptographically secured currencies would spread rapidly and become more widely used in the everyday world. They would become more prominent in the trading and investment environment, as well as more commonly used with transactions. Blockchain technology also has the ability to completely eliminate the need for centralized banks. Since the system is infinitely more secure and efficient, physical bank locations would cease to exist due to a floundering need for their presence. Still, the real risks associated with banks would remain present, even if the banks were to be transitioned over to the blockchain technologies.

Other amazing things associated with banks becoming involved in blockchain technologies is that the costs associated with securities trading, cross-border payments, and regulatory compliance could be greatly reduced. It would be much less costly for them to complete the transactions and therefore they could save as much as $20 billion by the year 2022. The number of applications that would be associated within' and outside of centralized banks would be greatly reduced, as well. Blockchain transactions would contain all relevant information for transfers to be successful, and therefore there would be no need for such a high volume of paperwork and contract signings to be associated with transactions.

Some people, however, do not see blockchain as being a positive. Some banks believe that this system could be dangerous as there simply isn't enough IT infrastructure available to support the system. If anything were ever to go wrong with it, there wouldn't be enough knowledgeable minds to fix it. Additionally, if the system was down for any amount of time, it would have the potential to be compromised and it would cause serious backlash on the markets. They believe that the blockchain system might just be the opportunity for another cartel to be opened and that it will be dominated by cryptocurrencies. These banks believe that blockchain would fail to be able to function effectively enough to operate everyday payments, which is a major part of banking for the majority of people.

Blockchain technology has the potential to completely change the face of financial infrastructure as we know it. Smart contracts, smart property, and other blockchain-based applications would completely change the way the systems functioned and there would be no need for existing methods to be used anymore. Ultimately, it could completely bypass the way our financial systems currently operate and change the face of the financial world entirely. Nothing would be untouched by the system, from trading and transactions to sales and everyday banking.

Many other industries would be greatly impacted by the blockchain systems, as well. While these industrial changes have not been as deeply explored as the financial industry's changes have been, they still exist. Ultimately, it will be up to those industries to really see how exactly blockchain systems can have an impact on their businesses. Still, it is inevitable that they will be directly affected by the system.

One way that blockchain is guaranteed to have an impact on various industries is through transaction processes. Virtually every industry has an underlying financial structure, and this structure will not be immune to the changes that blockchain will bring about. It is, however, believed that blockchain would have a highly positive impact on these industries. For example, these businesses would not have to rely on third parties to facilitate transactions within' their business. Instead, it would all be done through blockchain systems. This would completely change the face of business banking.

In addition to changing the financial structure of the business and the way transactions are facilitated, blockchain would have the ability to create entirely new business opportunities. Existing technologies and processes would be completely disrupted, but as a result, there would be entirely new opportunities available. People could use blockchain as a trading post, they could rent the excess cloud storage, and they could become trained as blockchain consultants to assist others in navigating the blockchain environment. There would be many other careers opened up too, as a result.

Blockchain would have the opportunity to completely shrink the world as we know it. The boundaries between countries and businesses would be completely eliminated. Transactions and trades across the board would be easier than ever to facilitate, and there would be much less difficulty when working with businesses from anywhere. Transactions would be instant and businesses could interact overseas just as effortlessly as they would if they were direct next-door neighbors.

Ultimately, the face of business would completely change. Models behind businesses would change, career opportunities would open up, and trading would become much easier. Businesses large and small would all have fair chances at the same opportunities, and there would be almost nothing keeping small businesses from having the same impact as large businesses currently do. Smaller businesses would be opened up to opportunities to have a major impact on the world and take their business from a local market to a global and universal market.

In addition to banks and business, blockchain would also have a massive impact on governments. If blockchain were to be completely integrated, traditional currencies as we know it could be eliminated entirely. Instead of having different currencies for different nations, we would have bitcoin and other cryptocurrencies that would dominate the market. There would be no need for country- or region-specific currencies. As well, blockchain would be an excellent way to distribute currencies to developing nations in order to assist in raising social welfare and ensuring that everyone across the globe was taken care of. We would be able to eliminate the boundaries and lines across countries and come together as one united global community.

Another powerful way that blockchain would have the ability to impact government is through elections. As we have already explored, blockchain could be used to eliminate the expenses and time investment in elections. Instead of having to fund expensive election facilities and hire and train the people to run them, everything could be done instantaneously online. This would increase the speed, improve voter turnout, and decrease the costs associated with elections.

The idea of self-driving cars, fridges that order and pay for food, and technology that can completely self-service itself was once a mere dream of a futuristic society. People dreamt up a vast number of incredible changes that society would endure if technology advanced to such a space, and in the meantime computer scientists, cryptographers and mathematicians were in the process of turning those dreams into a reality. Blockchain is the system that is bringing us forward into this futuristic society in the fastest way possible. Just a decade ago, blockchain was only a dream. It rapidly became a reality, however, and it continues to hurdle forward to be the new potential for our society. Time will only tell how far this blockchain revolution actually goes, but it is clear that it isn't about to stop anytime soon.

Chapter 8 Benefits of the Blockchain Technology

Other than being the backbone upon which cryptocurrencies such as Bitcoin rest, the blockchain technology has a vast number of uses whose benefits surpasses that of cryptocurrencies and their creation. Let us discuss some of these benefits before we discuss Ethereum in the next section.

The need for blockchain is not as evident as it would be because as many postulate, you can use a software or platform such as Google or databases to record transactions. While databases have no fault, blockchain has proven effectual and beneficial. Here are some of its key benefits:

Fully Distributed

This is one of the key benefits of the blockchain technology. As illustrated many times in this guide, participants in any blockchain application, perhaps Bitcoin mining or trading, will have access to a copy of the most current blockchain.

Mining of the currencies that use these technologies is also distributed. This means that at any point in time, no computer (no matter how powerful it is) can dominate the network. If that were the case, the most powerful computers would do all the mining and hog all the created currencies leaving none for the hobby miner. The distributed nature of the blockchain makes this impossible.

Use of Decentralized Verification

We have discussed how currencies and applications that use the blockchain technology are decentralized. This aspect of the innovation eliminates the need for a central authority such as a central bank; having to take transactions through a central database can be limiting in terms of the time it takes for the transaction to happen.

Enhanced Security

In a widely corrupt internet where some people use blackhat strategies to trick users into giving them their bank and credit card information, an anonymous way of paying for goods and services proves very helpful. Since many online buyers are seeking anonymity above all else, they are turning to blockchain powered currencies such as Bitcoins and Ether since these currencies use cryptographically secure, complex algorithms to record all transactions without compromising personal identity. To make and receive blockchain-powered currencies, all you need is an address. This reduces the risk of fraud.

Enhanced Trust among Parties

Blockchain offers top-level security features (using cryptographic code). This increases the level of trust between those transacting. Further, because there is zero exchange of value, and records of the transactions remain on the blockchain under all circumstances, the level of trust between those sending cryptocurrencies and those receiving it increases.

Low Entry Barrier

This is one of the key benefits of the blockchain innovation: it allows anyone to use the network—anyone who has an internet connected computer or smartphone can use blockchain and Bitcoins as long as he or she downloads the client software.

Real-time Transactional Capabilities

Waiting for three or more days for a transaction to reflect on your bank or account statement is a pain many users are keen to avoid whenever they can —today's consumers want immediate results after making any purchase: they want the transaction to reflect on their accounts almost immediately.

The blockchain technology makes it possible to make payments immediately or within 10 minutes, which when you consider the time it takes for credit cards to process transactions, is the best option currently available.

Enhanced Global Operations and Trade

Considering that we live in an interconnected world where someone in America can be in business with someone living at the farthest point in Africa, the need for speedy transactions has never been higher. Blockchain based currencies enhance this intercontinental trade by enhancing the speed of transactions and reducing the fees levied on sending monies from one person or business to the other.

Eliminates the Problem of Double Spending

This is something we discussed earlier as one of the key advantages of the blockchain technology. We have also mentioned that applications using the blockchain use cryptography to secure the system and prevent the duplication of transaction (especially monetary ones) to make sure that users of the system do not produce money out of thin air.

The system processes each transaction once before entering it into a block and linking the block to the chain. Once processed and recorded into the blockchain, the system cannot process that transaction again; this eliminates the redundancy so common with the records of most modern banking systems. Further, because the arrangement of the blocks uses a linear and chronological manner, tracking transactions becomes dummy-easy.

Low Transaction Costs

One of the main reasons why the uptake of cryptocurrencies such as Bitcoins and Litecoins has been on the rapid rise is the fact that most of these currencies have the lowest transfer rates imaginable. This plays in very well with consumers who are looking to save money on transactional fees as they shop.

The links below show how to calculate transactional fees for ether and Bitcoins.

https://ethereum.stackexchange.com/questions/19665/how-to-calculate-transaction-fee

https://en.bitcoin.it/wiki/Transaction_fees

https://bitcoinfees.21.co/

Those advocating for, and spearheading the use of, the blockchain technology are quick to point out that the applicability of the innovation goes beyond that of Bitcoin or financial transactions. For instance, many of those involved are quick to point out that the blockchain shall play an integral role in elections of the future (read more here).

Still, like every new technology, there are those who feel that the technology has its fair share of drawbacks, especially its ability to accommodate the rapid uptake and increased number of transactions. Since most applications that use this technology create an average of 61 new blocks every 10 minutes, each individual system creates an average of 144 blocks per day. To the cautious, this is something they consider problematic because it may influence the storage and speed of transaction, which may lead to update and synchronization issues.

Let us flesh out some of the drawbacks of the blockchain technology and discuss their possible solutions:

Chapter 9 Disadvantages of Using Blockchain Technology

While the blockchain has many uses and an immense number of benefits, it also has its drawbacks. In this subsection, we shall look at these disadvantages as well as how to overcome them:

Performance

The first issue many are quick to point out is the issue of performance. Some experts in the field of finance point out that compared to the speed of centralized databases especially in relation to transaction records, the blockchain is slower because on top of recording a transaction as a normal database does, it also has to do three other things:

1.   Verify signature: Every blockchain transaction must have a digital signature that uses a public-private cryptographic scheme (a good example is the ECDSA signature). Without this signature, it would be impossible to prove the source of transactions propagated on the nodes of the peer-to-peer network. As you can guess, generating and verifying these signatures requires a massive amount of computer power and, since the signatures are complex, their computation may take time thus slowing down the recording of transactions. In comparison, centralized databases (normal ones) do not have to contend with this problem because after the establishment of a connection with the databases, it eliminates the need for individual verification of requests coming over it.

Possible solution: A possible solution for this is the move to proof-of-stake, which would make transactions faster while eliminating the need to have nodes on the network verify individual transactions.

2.   Consensus Mechanism: One of the key characteristic of the blockchain is that it monitors the nodes (computers) on the network and, using some of the computing power of the network, makes sure the nodes within the network reach consensus. Achieving this consensus means there has to be a significant back-and-forth communication between all the nodes and may involve dealing with forks and their effects on the blockchain. This may cause a slowdown of transaction procession. While traditional centralized databases also have to contend with aborted and conflicting transactions, because the database is centralized, these are few.

Possible solution: The consensus mechanism is all about proof-of-work. As the system moves away from proof-of-work to proof-of-stake, it is bound to remove the hindrances that come with it.

The links below detail critical information about the various consensus mechanisms used by various blockchain applications:

https://www.linkedin.com/pulse/types-consensus-mechanism-used-blockchain-munish-singh/

https://bitmalta.com/blockchain-consensus/

3.   Redundancy: In this regard, redundancy does not necessarily mean the performance of individual nodes on the network; it means the amount of computing power required to compute a blockchain. Every node on the blockchain network must process every node individually, something that does not plague centralized databases that process individual transactions just ones. On the blockchain network, this means

more work for the same results, which as you can guess, leads to slowed down processes.

Possible solution: Again, most blockchain application and technologies use proof-of-work to verify transactions. A move to proof-of-stake and other consensus mechanism would eliminate this and take with it the drawbacks.

To learn more about the average time it takes the blockchain network to record transactions, read the insightful content on the links below.

https://coincenter.org/entry/how-long-does-it-take-for-a-bitcoin-transaction-to-be-confirmed

https://bitcoin.stackexchange.com/questions/7323/how-long-does-it-take-on-average-to-receive-one-confirmation-is-it-still-revers

Energy

Many have touted the blockchain technology as the answer to global warming because it provides a transparent currency not based on consumption. Some opine that the innovation as currently instituted — where computer nodes spread across the world have to record all transaction using proof-of-work — leaves a massive carbon imprint because all the computers on the network have to use energy. In fact, some experts are quick to point out that the peer-to-peer power used to process Bitcoins is superior to that of the world's fastest computers combined.

Possible Solution: A possible solution to this is to move away from proof-of-work, thereby eliminating the need for mining, and move to other consensus mechanisms that do not require combined computing power. While this solution may not be forthcoming anytime soon, it shall, and when it does, it shall change everything.

The other solution is a tradeoff between security and size where those spearheading the development of the technology can trade security for size. The downside to this is that the more nodes you have on the network, the more secure it is; however, in an instance where you only want part of the data on the blockchain, perhaps having a smaller, yet faster network would be better. This means that institutions such as banks can set up their smaller blockchain networks and by so doing, save on energy costs, and increase the rate of transaction recording.

Interoperability

Interoperability, making sure that the network and the data therein has standards and is not a bunch of stuff, is a growing concern. Since blockchain technology is open-source and anyone can use it to create whatever blockchain application he or she wants while tweaking it accordingly, there are no set standards for the technology, and competing blockchain platforms are free to use it as they wish. The individual changes and tweaks make it impossible for competing blockchain technologies to achieve a level of interoperability.

Possible solution: A possible solution for this would be for all blockchain-based app developers to achieve consensus and make their individual blockchain applications compatible with the wider web; they can do this by integrating their apps into existing processes and practices.

Privacy

Although most applications using the blockchain technology as their backbone use cryptography to secure data, privacy is a key concern since the blockchain is a publicly visible ledger. This level of openness is not what anyone would consider the most secure way to store sensitive data.

As an example, the Bitcoin blockchain/database has a record of all transactions ever conducted on the platform. This data is open for all to see, which also means anyone can use the same data against someone else. A case in point is the Department of Work and Pension. In May 2016, they started using the blockchain to track how claimants use their benefits.

When you consider that when you conduct transactions over the Bitcoin blockchain, you are publishing your bank statement online for all to see, privacy concerns are sure to arise.

Possible Solution: A possible solution for this would be to use complex cryptographic code to make sure that the transactions are secure and no one can game the system or use the information therein to disadvantage someone else. Another possible solution would be Bitcoin mixing.

The following link has some great ideas on how to enhance privacy over the Bitcoin blockchain (the principles also apply to other blockchain technologies).

https://coinsutra.com/anonymous-bitcoin-transactions/

Changing Truths

The blockchain operates on the premise that all information recorded into it is eternal truth and shall remain so. Reality, as you very well know, is greyer than that. In fact, some jurisdictions such as the EU and the UK have laws detailing the right to be forgotten. For instance, in the UK, if you change your gender, it is your right to have the same reflect all through history (records of birth, baptism, etc.).

If a governmental institution that offers governmental services such as birth records uses a blockchain ledger, that would mean changing such information would be impossible and doing so would lead to the creation of a fork, as was the case with the DAO project.

Encryption

One of the main points we have impressed repeatedly is that most applications on the blockchain technology use cryptography to encrypt information. This encryption creates a number of issues. For one, anyone with a key — perhaps a super user such as the person responsible for creating the specific blockchain application, someone who knows its inner working modalities — can access the encrypted data (so can anyone if the key becomes public). The other issue is that if someone loses the key that unlocks the blockchain, that blockchain would be worthless and difficult, if not impossible to get back.

As the hack on the DAO project proved, encryption, no matter how strong it is, is vulnerable either through the exploitation of backdoors and loopholes, or using new technologies. For instance, even with the immense power of peer-to-peer computing, a technology such as quantum computing (once developed), can knock the bejeezus out of the peer-to-peer network and overpower it, thus making it vulnerable. Therefore, saying we can use cryptography to encrypt the data in the blockchain may not be enough in itself since people will always be looking for ways to de-encrypt encrypted data.

Possible Solution: A possible solution for this would be to make sure that the key that unlocks an encrypted blockchain does not fall into the wrong hands (meaning it should not be public, which in itself presents a problem seeing how the blockchain is an open ledger).

Another solution for this is to implement strong privacy protection laws and strategies. The link below has some invaluable insight into this:

https://github.com/ethereum/wiki/wiki/Problems

Illegal Entries

Consider an instance where someone with malicious intent embeds illegal data into a blockchain. That would make the entire blockchain illegal. It would also mean that anyone on the blockchain would be guilty of breaking the law and therefore culpable.

For instance, James Smith, ODI's Head of Labs Programme and co-author of a report named 'Applying Blockchain Technology in Global Data Infrastructure,' added an illegal encryption key for HD DVD on the PlayStation to the blockchain. To date, no one cares about this and the blockchain upon which the illegal encryption key rests is on everyone's' machine.

Discovering Information

The blockchain database has in place ways to record data (through the computation power of the nodes on the network). However, usage of the data is not as easy since to use the data, you have to find the data you intend to use.

While it is possible to index the blockchain into searchable databases, finding specific information in a reliable manner would require that those participating in the network have the same blockchain history stored on their nodes and a capable search index built from this blockchain. Achieving a distributed search index is something the technology is yet to explore.

Possible solution: A possible solution for information discovery would be to have one site having a search index for the chain. This may lead to possible issues as well since not many would be willing to trust that one site. The lasting solution would be to integrate a capable search feature into the blockchain.

The following links list a number of other blockchain related problems and their possible solutions:

https://appliedblockchain.com/outstanding-challenges-in-blockchain-2017/

https://www.coindesk.com/information/blockchains-issues-limitations/

https://www.kaspersky.com/blog/bitcoin-blockchain-issues/18019/

https://techcrunch.com/2016/02/03/lets-be-honest-about-the-problems-with-blockchain-and-finance/

Now that we have hashed out the possible shortcomings of the blockchain, let us discuss Ethereum, the other blockchain technology that is taking the world by storm and after that, discuss how you can start using the blockchain.

Chapter 10 The Role of Blockchain Technology in Future Capital Markets

Blockchain technology has caused a real stir, particularly in the financial world. Many banks, venture capitalists, and other financial institutions are already looking into how blockchain technology can be used to store data and for other financial uses. One such financial industry is capital markets and it is here that the industry experts are showing the most enthusiasm and optimism about using blockchain technology to solve a number of issues.

Asset Movement

In order for assets to be moved from one financial institution to another, the ledger balances for the assets must also move. This is not an easy job and involves the use of several intermediaries. The more there are involved in the transaction, the more messages need to be exchanged and this results in even more updating of the ledgers required. In an average trade, there are already several intermediaries, including CCPs (central counterparties), exchanges, CSDs (central securities depositories, custodians, brokers and investment managers. In order for the accounting to be correct and for the transaction to be successfully completed, all of the intermediaries involved have to make sure their ledgers are updated based on the messages that are exchanged.

In essence, this means that whenever a transaction takes place, even more messaging needs to be carried out and this causes delays and adds to the total cost. On occasion, in order for a transaction to be completed and all the correct ledger updates made, the intermediaries may have to complete even more ledgers, such as securities borrowing, realignments or cash management. All this does is delay the transaction and is usually referred to, in capital market speak, as a settlement cycle.

So how can blockchain technology help? The creation of a shared flat ledger to process the transactions that happen between several intermediaries is the most important expectation of the capital market industry and will help in cutting both the time and the costs involved in each transaction. Using blockchain technology will also ensure that real-time asset transfers can easily be facilitated.

Financial industries can make use of blockchain technology to build shared flat ledgers that can easily be managed by processing nodes that are trusted. Through the use of digital signatures, the intermediaries will be able to update the ledgers to finish the business transaction. Shared ledgers have to be encrypted so that data confidentiality is maintained. The key processes that are involved in the execution of a trade, like trading, security clearance, settlement and clearing can easily be redesigned and made much simpler with the use of the blockchain.

Onboarding and Maintenance

Account maintenance and client onboarding is the next part of the capital market industry where blockchain technology is highly likely to be put to good use. KYC, or Know Your Customer, costs are incredibly high and cutting down on the cost and cutting out some of the KYC checks that need to be done is just what business the world over are looking to do. If they had a system built in the blockchain that both stored and facilitated Know Your Customer data, they can cut their costs and they can cut down on the amount of YC checks that need to be done. There are already a number of blockchain startup businesses that are focused on the improvement of identity management and we expect to see this number rise significantly over the coming years.

What About Payments?

Payments are a segment of the market where we can expect to see a substantial rise in the use of blockchain technology over the next few years. The blockchain technology can be used to customize the business rules for the processing of transactions, as well as help to tailor these rules to the specific business. This will all be based on the needs of the specific organization and the technology used would be open source software, enabling any number of businesses to use and tailor the software to their own requirements.

Areas that will see the biggest benefits of blockchain technology are bonds trading and OTC (over the counter) derivatives. The technology will be able to provide the business with a secure settlement model that is in real-time and is also cost effective to run, along with being decentralized and global. In short, it really is just a matter of time before the blockchain steps in and starts playing an immense role in capital markets.

A financial services company, based in Belgium and called Euroclear explains how blockchain technology can help the capital market sector. They say that, put basically, the records for every security would be placed onto a flat accounting basis, which means there would be "multiple levels of beneficial ownership" contained on each ledger. There would no more need to operating data normalization for reconciling internal systems or for agreements on exposure and obligation. There would be processes and services that are standardized, reference data would be shared, processing capabilities, like reconciliations, would be standardized, data would be near real-time and there would be a better understanding of the worthiness of counterparts. For regulators and other privileged participants, there would be better transparency on holdings data, along with a whole host of other improvements.

The Benefits for the Capital Market

According to Euroclear, the capital market segment would reap the following benefits:

Pre-Trade

- Better transparency of holdings
- Better verification of holding
- A reduction in credit exposures
- Mutualization of all static data
- Much easier KYC

Trade

- More secure transaction matching in real-time
- Immediate and irrevocable settlement of transactions
- Automatic cash ledger DVP
- Automatic reporting
- Better, more transparent supervision for the market authorities
- Higher standards in AML2

Post-Trade

- Real-time cash transactions do not need to go through central clearing

- Reduced margin requirements
- Reduced collateral requirements
- Interchangeable use of assets as collateral on the blockchain
- Automatic execution of all smart contracts

Securities Servicing and Custody

- Primary proceedings directly to the blockchain
- Automation of servicing processes
- De-duplication of servicing processes
- Better central datasets that have flat accounting orders
- Common data for reference
- Automatic processing of fund subscriptions and redemption directly on the blockchain
- More simplified method of fund servicing
- More simplified method of accounting
- Simpler methods of administration and allocation

Who are the Early Believers and the Pioneers of the Blockchain Technology?

On the Public Platform

1. NASDAQ - In December of 2015, NASDAQ released an official statement to say that Linq, its own blockchain ledger technology, had been successful in completing and recording a private securities transaction. This was the very first time this had been achieved using blockchain. NASDAQ Linq is a digital

ledger that uses the blockchain to aid in the cataloging, issuance and recording of shares that are held in the Private Market by privately held companies. It is designed to complement the cloud-based capitalization management that NASDAQ Private Market, called ExactEquity. Linq clients will be given a full historical and comprehensive record of the issue and transfer of their own securities, providing much better auditability, governance of issue and transfer of ownership.

2. ASX – the ASX is the largest stock exchange in Australia and it has now confirmed that it is working on the development of a private blockchain in conjunction with Digital Asset, a US-based firm, as a solution for post-trade in the Equity market in Australia. The ASX paid a sum of AUD $14.9 million to gain an equity interest of 5% in Digital Assets Holdings and this fee will be used to fund the first phase of the distributed ledger solution.

On the Private Platform

1. Chain.com – Chain is a blockchain startup that documents the use of the NASDAQ technology to issue shares to a private investor. The issuer of the securities used NASDAQ Linq to represent, in the digital sense, a record of ownership. The settlement time was reduced significantly and the paper stock certificates were, in effect, redundant. Linq also allows investors and issuers to complete subscription documents and then execute them, all online.

2. Funderbeam – this company is set to launch the very first investment trading platform that is based on the blockchain technology in the next few months. They will be doing this through a partnership with ChromaWay, a developer of colored coins. Each of the syndicates will be paired up with a micro fund and that micro fund will own real stakes in real startups. As such, when a member of the

syndicate wants to trade some or all of their own holdings, they will actually be trading digital stakes in the micro fund. The blockchain will be used to verify every transaction before it is enforced and the same thing happens when an investor decides to sell all or part of their digital stakes. In each of the investments, the change of ownership will have a distributed audit trail that is fully secure.

The Challenges Faced by the Capital Market in Adopting Blockchain Technology

The capital market will face a number of challenges that they will need to overcome if blockchain technology is to be adopted successfully:

1.   There must be very high standards set for the technology to succeed. This is mainly for the security, for the performance and the robustness of the blockchains. Also, non-blockchain systems, like risk management platforms, will also have to be integrated at some point in the near future.

2.   Legislation and Regulations Must Be Upgraded. In order for blockchain technologies to be successfully made an integral part of the infrastructure, new regulatory principles will need to be fully integrated.

3.   New Standards and Governance Will Be Required. On some design points, industry alignment will be a requirement. Some of those points include whether the systems in use are fully open, like the bitcoin system, or whether they use a system of permission-based access; the principles that govern whether the system is suitable for interaction with the ledger; whether different systems are interoperable – systems may be running difference safeguards against errors in coding or consensus protocols and this could create knock-on effects that may not be detectable to start with

4. The Proper Management of the Transition to Minimize Operational Risk. Operational risk is a big consideration and it must be minimized as far as possible.

Blockchain Companies Already Applying Distributed Ledger Security

These companies have already built their systems and are applying the blockchain-based distributed ledger technology to security and compliance

1. Third-Key Solutions – They provide cryptographic key management solutions and consulting to companies who use distributed blockchains, decentralized digital currencies and asset tokens

2. Chainalysis – provides products that let financial institutions spot the connections between two or more digital identities and develop lines of trust between them. The products can also help them to identify any malicious actors in the process. Chainalysis states that their mission is to come up with tools that stop any abuse of the system they are being applied to and that respect the privacy of users.

3. Tradle – uses the blockchain to bridge external and internal financial networks to achieve portability in KYC that is controlled by the user. An open-source mobile framework has been combined with business app development and a full integration platform that allows Tradle to develop sophisticated full-stack blockchain apps

4. Vogogo – This company specializes in providing verification tools for both payment processing and for risk management. To do this they use a simple JSON REST API.

5. Elliptic – the first company in the world to secure blockchain asset insurance and to achieve accreditation from

one of the Big Four Audit firms, KPMG. They offer AML bitcoin protection in real-time

6. Civic – an identity solution that is based on the blockchain, aiming to tackle consumer identity theft and to bring about a reduction in online identity fraud.

7. Coinalytics – this company allows enterprises to determine real-time risk assessment and intelligence from the decentralized applications and from blockchains. They use methodologies that are based on pattern recognition and on real-time learning online to mine simulated data with few features.

8. Sig3 – The company uses multi-sig technology to provide extra security layers for transactions made through bitcoin Instead of a requirement for just one signature or one key to make a transaction, the user is able to set up a multi-sig wallet requiring the signature from two of three provided keys before the transaction can be completed and broadcast to the blockchain network. Because Sig3 is an independent automated third-party co-signer, it can be integrated into any multi-sig wallet while maintaining distance from said wallet. This ensures there is no point of failure.

9. Blockseer - This company has a mission to build a "unified foundation of transparency" for the public ecosystem for bitcoin. By providing the transparency of the blockchain and all of its participants, the company is aiming to cut down on the disorder and chaos and increase knowledge levels and analysis of the public blockchain network

10. CryptoCorp – This company is a security startup that is focused entirely on bringing about improvements to the bitcoin ecosystem. They offer a service

that is called Digital Oracle, which can take part in multi-signature transactions that originate from any bitcoin wallet

11. Blockverify – A company that offers an anti-counterfeit system that is based on the blockchain. The system can be applied to luxury items, pharmaceuticals, diamonds and electronics and, using Blockverify, companies will be able to create their own product registers and monitor their own supply chains.

Chapter 11 Building a Mining Rig

Mining Basics

Thousands of computers all over the planet mine cryptocurrencies, and many of these computers are doing so because of viruses designed specifically for mining. If you have ever had your computer slow down because of a virus, it is possible that a miner was installed on your computer.

The reason that someone would design a virus to do disturbed mining is because the component costs to mining are the cost of the hardware and the cost to power the hardware. A virus bypasses both of these costs so that the creator of the virus can only profit. Even so, it is unlikely that the creator of a virus that mines cryptocurrencies has made a tremendous sum of money.

You need very specific hardware to mine cryptocurrencies at an efficient rate. In this chapter you will learn about all of the parts that you will need to build your own mining rig. It might seem like a monumental task, but the truth is that getting a mining rig off the ground is a relatively simple process.

All you need to do is select the parts and build it yourself, or barring that ask for help from a local computer store to help you assemble the parts – this was the avenue I took for my first mining rig, and along with paying for assembly I also paid to learn how to build future rigs by myself.

The key to successful cryptocurrency mining is to buy parts that are power efficient and capable of mining at a fast rate. Since these computers are designed for a singular purpose, there are many standard parts that you will not need. They are also based around desktop parts as these are cheaper, but they also allow for larger graphics processing units (GPU) – the basis for mining efficiently.

The reason that a virus will not be able to mine efficiently, even when on thousands of computers, is that most personal computers today are laptops. Laptops have a central processing unit (CPU) that handles the standard calculations, but also renders all the video and images that you see on your computer monitor.

The fact of the matter is that running calculations on a CPU is incredibly inefficient. A moderately powered graphics card will be able to mine at a far greater rate than even ten or twenty decently powered laptops.

It is important that as you build your mining rig that you spend money on the parts that are important, and minimize the costs on superfluous items. For example, you will not need computer monitors, keyboards and mice or speakers for these computers.

Ideally they do not have more than the parts necessary for efficient mining. You will of course need one monitor and a single keyboard and mouse to set up the mining on machines, but once the setup is complete the rest is handled automatically.

Motherboard

Assembling a modern computer might seem terrifying, but the truth is that it is quite similar to assembling Lego. Each part is a block that plugs into a central board called the 'motherboard'. This base component is where you will put your CPU/GPU and all of the other components that make up your computer. A motherboard is a necessary part, but not one that you should be spending all that much money on.

Even relatively inexpensive motherboards will serve fine for the purposes of mining. The most important aspect is that you buy a motherboard that is full size, as opposed to micro. The main consideration here is heat, and a smaller board does not fare as well as a larger one.

You can expect a motherboard to cost between $50 and $80, with preferable brands being ASUS, GIGABYTE and MSI. What's important is that your motherboard will be a determining factor in the type of central processing unit that you will use.

There are two main suppliers of processors, AMD and Intel. Depending on the motherboard, you will need the corresponding slot type and manufacturer. For example, an Intel LGA1155 board will only take Intel processors of that socket type. Do not let 'LGA1155' scare you – simply put, marketers have not realized the usefulness of catchy names for computer parts.

I strongly urge you to go with an Intel based motherboard capable of fitting an i3 or i5 processor. AMD processors are simply worse at handling heat, which is one of your main concerns for reducing the overhead cost of running a mining rig. You may first want to look at your choices of CPU and then base your motherboard decision off of what processor you will be purchasing.

As a general rule of thumb, processor costs are more fixed than motherboards. You may find an excellent sale on a motherboard, but it unlikely that the cost of a processor will change. Typically the manufacturer of CPUs will issue parts and never adjust the prices, only modifying pricing when new models of processors come out.

You should note that a motherboard will have many components already built into it. For example, your networking capability should be built into your motherboard. This is where you will also find your audio outputs and inputs for keyboard and mouse.

Power Supply

The power supply is the most important component of a mining rig. I have heard countless stories of people buying a cheap power supply only to see their mining rig burst into flames. This is not meant to be alarmist – power supplies are very safe, but they range in build quality greater than any other part on this list. The power supply is so essential because the computer will be running twenty-four hours a day, so stability is key.

I would recommend an EVGA, Thermaltake, or CORSAIR power supply. They come in different wattages, but for your needs, you must simply look for one that is 400 watts or greater. You should also note that power supplies are graded in terms of quality. Provided you buy a power supply that is silver or gold rated, you will be fine.

Additionally, the manufactures I have listed only make high quality power supplies, so even a bronze rated EVGA power supply will be sufficient. Expect the cost of a power supply to range between $50 and $80, depending on sales and promotions.

Power supplies should be changed out every eighteen months. All power supplies fail; the question is merely a matter of time, and how they will die. A poorly manufactured power supply will take all of the connected parts with it, meaning that an entire rig can be lost. A well-made power supply will simply stop working, meaning you can salvage all of the parts in the machine. You would simply need to replace the power supply to get it running again.

Since these machines are running at maximum load all of the time, an eighteen month period of use is to be expected. You can run them for longer, but you always risk a failure that may take out other parts with it.

Graphics Card (GPU)

The graphics card is the second most important part of your mining rig. This is where the true computational power comes into play. While a central processing unit can only handle a few calculations at a time, a graphics card can handle hundreds at the same time. It is a byproduct of their design, taking instructions from the CPU to power onscreen images. The relative power in each core of the GPU is low, but with so many of them they can mine much more efficiently than any CPU.

There are two main brands to buy from for graphics processors, NVidia and AMD. This is the same AMD that also makes CPUs, and for what it is worth the other main CPU manufacturer, Intel, owns NVidia. Both companies have good models of consumer video cards for mining. Most recently both companies have released new products that consume less power and are more efficient when it comes to heat.

There is a bit of a trade off in these two manufacturers. NVidia costs a bit more, and is not as fast as similar AMD cards, however they are more reliable overall, consume less power and produce drastically less heat. For my own rigs, I primarily use NVidia cards. This is merely because their cards were available to me before the latest line of AMD cards.

I would recommend that you either use a NVidia 1060 ($250) or an AMD 480 ($200). Both of these models have variations depending on the manufacturer of the card. For example you may see an EVGA 480, but this is the same base product as the one that AMD offers.

Without getting into too many details, the boards are free to be manufactured provided the companies get royalties for the technology. The primary difference is sometimes the clock speeds are increased, or the mounted cooling units are more efficient. There is no brand of either GPU that I would not recommend, and in fact I would just go with whatever is cheapest.

In these various models you will also see that they are differentiated based on the amount of memory that they have, coming in 3 and 6 GB versions for NVidia, and 4 and 8 GB versions for AMD. For the purposes of mining, the onboard video memory does not matter – buy the card with less memory as it will always be cheaper.

A GPU should be replaced once every two to three years, but the main catalyst for replacement should be that a new and more efficient model has been released. When a GPU dies, it simply stops working, so the build quality is not as essential as with a power supply.

It is my recommendation that if you start building mining rigs, you on occasion look at benchmarks for power efficiency in video cards. New cards come out roughly every year or so, with major revisions happening every two to four years – the latest major revisions were in 2016.

Central Processing Unit (CPU)

For processors you have a choice between Intel and AMD. What processor type you buy does not matter that much, as both are equally suitable for mining. What is important is that the socket type of the processor matches the motherboard that you buy. With this, it is my advice that you buy your motherboard and CPU at the same time, if only to ensure compatibility.

Like with video cards, the differences between the types of CPUs come down to heat and cost. AMD costs less but produces more heat. Intel costs more but produces less heat. Remember that more heat means more power consumption, and so you can trade the upfront cost for long term savings by going with Intel, or you can pay less now and go with AMD.

This is one of the more expensive parts of a mining rig, with the average cost of a processor being slightly over $200. The naming convention of the AMD processors is not as intuitive as the Intel system. I would suggest an i3 processor for Intel, which could cost as low as $150, or any AMD processor that is 'Bulldozer' or newer.

The upper limit for the cost of this part is $250, with the cheapest processor type coming in at $150. Other guides may suggest going with an i5 Intel processor, but the truth is that you don't really need this type of power. We are building a mining rig for home use, not a rig that will be joined with hundreds of other computers in a warehouse.

Memory (RAM)

The random access memory, or RAM, is a part that should not cost you more than $40 or $50. There are many different manufacturers of RAM, and I cannot recommend one brand over any other; that is because there is a consistent quality to RAM, which has more or less made it a commodity. You will need between 4 and 8 GB of system ram for efficient mining. 4 GB is fine in 2017, but by 2018 or 2019 you will likely want to have 8GB of RAM in your system.

This is an easily upgradeable part, so I would buy the cheapest and smallest amount as you get started. Please note that while the numbers and markings are the same, system RAM is very different from video card memory. One does not substitute the other, so even if you have a 3 GB video card, you will still need 4 GB of system RAM for your rig.

Storage

Storage is an essential part of any computer, but not one that you should spend a lot of money on. Storage options come in the form of hard drives (HDD) and solid state drives (SSD), with the latter being far more expensive. There has been a push for miners to move to SSD due to the lower power usage, but I have found the cost of SSDs to be so great that the upfront cost does not justify the long term power usage.

Any hard drive from any manufacturer will do – look for storage sizes of 80 GB up to 1 TB, and buy whatever part is cheapest. Note that hard drives do fail and that without a storage drive your rig will stop working. You will need to replace it if it fails, but you will not lose any of your cryptocurrency, as that is stored on the public ledger and not locally on your machine.

Operating System

Your options for operating systems are Windows or Linux, and I highly recommend the later. A Linux license is free and an image can be found online quite easily. To install an operating system like Linux, simply create a bootable flash drive by following the instructions provided by the specific version of Linux that you install. I would recommend Linux Red Hat or Ubuntu – you can think of these naming conventions as Windows 7, 10 etc.

They all have the same foundation but their interface is slightly different. Before you decide on the version of Linux that you want, I do suggest that you look at a compatibility chart to ensure your preferred cryptocurrency is listed. Once you have Linux installed, you must simply download the cryptocurrency client that you wish to mine. Install the client, set up an account and follow the instructions to start mining.

Chapter 12 Blockchain Technology Myths

It is very clear that the technology behind the blockchain is going to be the most important computing invention of this generation. This is because, for the very first time in the history of the human being, we have a full digital exchange for peer-to-peer value. Blockchain is a massive global platform and is firmly based on distributed ledger. It is responsible for establishing the rules, in the format of very heavy encryption and computations, that let at least two parties carry out transactions without the need for a centralized third party agency involved to establish the trust between the parties.

Instead of being reliant on government agencies, banks or any other intermediary to create that trust, the technology that fuels the blockchain ensures that trust is provided through clever doing and collaboration on a mass scale. The trust is actually built into the blockchain system and that is why the blockchain is otherwise known as "The Trust Protocol".

If we wanted to take that a step further, the blockchain plays several other roles. It is:

- An accounts ledger
- A database
- A sentry
- A clearing house

It is, in all likelihood, going to be the second-generation internet and it has the potential to take the economic grid and rewire it to run things for the better, shaking up the old and bringing in a completely new way of working. A fresh perspective on old business systems.

Sadly, there are still a lot of myths about blockchain technology doing the rounds and these are responsible for putting a lot of influential businesses and people off of using it. Here are the top 5 of those blockchain myths, busted and explained:

1.   Blockchain is good but bitcoin is bad

There are an awful lot of people, particularly in the financial sector that are very excited about the potential that blockchain technology provides. However, those same people are under the misconception that digital currencies are not feasible, they are not desirable and are in fact quite dangerous.

The blockchain for bitcoin is a permission less system, which means that anyone is able to get into it through a device that has internet access and can interact with it in the same way they do the internet. Blockchains that are permissioned, on the other hand, require that all users have specific credentials, such as an operator's license for the blockchain they want to access, and those credentials are provided by a governing body or by the members of the blockchain. These permissioned systems use the distributed ledger technology but do not have any digital currency attached to them.

At first look, the permissioned or private blockchain looks like having several advantages. For a start, members of the chain are able to make changes to the rules if they want to. They are only required to get the group they are a part of to agree to make the change, rather than having to get an entire network involved. Costs are reduced because the transactions only have to be validated by the chain members, not by that massive network. All of this can also help reduce the costs of electricity, benefitting the environments and regulators are likely to prefer them over and over the public chain, like bitcoin, because there is no need to anonymity.

But, there are some things to consider. If it is easy to change rules, it is easy to flaunt those same rules. When you limit freedoms intentionally, neutrality can be severely inhibited. If the open value innovation goes, the blockchain technology will do nothing more than stagnate and vulnerabilities will open up in it. The bitcoin blockchain, on the other hand, and any other that is tied to digital currencies, include incentives built in to encourage users to validate the transactions.

2. The financial services are the only real industry that will benefit from blockchains

Provided they are able to locate the right leadership, the FSI can alter itself using the technology behind blockchain. That technology has the potential to completely revolutionize financial services, from the humble bank account and debit card right up to the entire credit card network. If everyone is sharing the same distributed ledger, transaction settlements can happen straight away for everyone. Banks could use blockchain technology to speed up the system process and reduce the massive costs they face every day. The smartest of them will strategically use the technology, and that includes the permission less system, to get into newer markets and bring a whole bunch of new services out.

But the FSI is only a small part of the whole system. Blockchains have the potential to disrupt those that are already seen as the disrupters, like Uber. Blockchains will be at the very center of the IoT (Internet of Things) and will allow the smart device to contract with, carry out transactions and share data securely peer-to-peer.

The blockchain has the potential to completely reinvent how democracy works by ensuring that politicians have to do something they are not used to doing – be accountable to the public.

3.   Blockchains are B2B (business to business) and not for the general public

So many people are convinced that blockchain technology will turn around the economy and shake up our day to day life in more ways than we could imagine. They are not just for businesses, as others believe; the blockchain will have an effect on every man, woman and child in the world today.

4.   There are too many issues with blockchains to make them work

There are those who say that blockchain technology really isn't ready for the world yet. It's too difficult to use properly and the best applications are still growing, still being developed. There are others who say that there is a huge amount of energy required to get consensus across the network. They ask what would happen when millions of blockchains all connected, are processing untold numbers of transactions every day. Are there sufficient incentives in place to get people to take part and not try to overthrow the entire network? Could blockchain possibly be the biggest killer of jobs for people of all time? Instead of seeing these are bad reasons for taking on the technology, we should perhaps be looking at them as challenges of implementing the system.

5.   Satoshi Nakamoto is actually Craig Wright

Craig Wright is an Australian entrepreneur who has sensationally claimed that he is the original inventor of the bitcoin, Satoshi Nakamoto. We already know that Satoshi is the only creator; there were others involved. When the first bitcoin paper was written, and the first protocol, that was what got things started. Then that person disappeared off the scene, leaving the community to keep the work going. It is that community that is responsible for most of the blockchain code and all other bitcoin-related content. In that case, everyone in the community is actually Satoshi.

This is why it doesn't really matter who the original protocol. It is a permission less system and that means there will never be an arbitrator. For the next step to be taken, the entire community has to be the governor for things to move forward. The likelihood of Craig Wright being the real Satoshi Nakamoto is very slim though

Conclusion

There is little doubt that blockchain technology will greatly change the global economy in coming years. From revamping the way that information is shared across organizations, to possibly being the underlying technology for a government issued cryptocurrency, the strength of blockchain lies in its ability to force cooperation among many disparate parties.

You are now well aware of where the future is heading, and what you can expect from the future of blockchain technology. You also have a firm understanding of how cryptocurrencies work, and how you can make a profit by mining them yourself.

I compiled the material in this book based on a single idea, for the reader to educate him or herself on blockchain and to make an impact on that reader's life. I hope that you feel enlightened about the nature of blockchain, and that you find some of the same amazement that I have over the years, about the genius of its creation and the interesting nature of its creators. It is truly an invention of the Internet era; a technology to restore power to the people.

By spreading information without a central institution or authority, blockchain democratizes information in much the same way the Internet originally did. It serves as a platform for services, ranging from databases to currencies, but its uses will grow far greater than anything we have seen in its current form today.

The last chapter of this book is dedicated to the idea of mining cryptocurrencies for profit. I know that for some readers this idea will seem fanciful, as if it is reserved for only the most technically inclined. I want to assure you that the only thing necessary to mine cryptocurrencies is the motivation and desire for profit. I came to blockchain technology purely out of fascination, but as I learned and started to understand how blockchain works, I have found that mining is a simple process that can be used to supplement your income.

I urge you to consider building your own mining rig; the cost of investment is low, and the potential for profit is unlimited. A mining rig is a platform to generate profit for many years into the future. While it is true that the exact amount of profit is unknown, cryptocurrencies have proven to be overall resilient enough that they are worth the investment.

Thank you and good luck!

www.ingramcontent.com/pod-product-compliance
Lightning Source LLC
Chambersburg PA
CBHW070211230526
45471CB00002B/920